Combating Teen Anxiety

Teen-Parent Communication Journal

Gina Nelson, LCSW

Copyright © 2022 by GINA NELSON, LCSW
All rights reserved.

No part of this publication may be reproduced, stored in a retrieval system, or transmitted in any form or by any means, electronic, mechanical, photocopying, recording, scanning, or otherwise, without the prior written permission of the author.

Limit of Liability/Disclaimer of Warranty: While the publisher and author have used their best efforts in preparing this book, they make no representations or warranties with respect to the accuracy or completeness of the contents of this book and specifically disclaim any implied warranties of merchantability or fitness for a particular purpose. No warranty may be created or extended by sales representatives or written sales materials. The advice and strategies contained herein may not be suitable for your situation. You should consult with a professional when appropriate. Neither the publisher nor the author shall be liable for any loss of profit or any other commercial damages, including but not limited to special, incidental, consequential, personal, or other damages.

COMBATING TEEN ANXIETY
Teen-Parent Communication Journal
by Gina Nelson, LCSW
FAM043000 - FAMILY & RELATIONSHIPS / Life Stages / Teenagers
JNF053050 - JUVENILE NONFICTION / Social Topics / Emotions & Feelings
PSY002000 - PSYCHOLOGY / Developmental / Adolescent
ISBN: 978-1-949642-89-6 (paperback)
978-1-949642-90-2 (ebook)

Cover design by LEWIS AGRELL

Printed in the United States of America

Authority Publishing
11230 Gold Express Dr. #310-413
Gold River, CA 95670
800-877-1097
www.AuthorityPublishing.com

This Journal Belongs To

_____

Teen

and

_____

Parent

About This Journal

Congratulations on your purchase of this journal. You are one step closer to learning to communicate more effectively with your anxious teen. As a Licensed Clinical Social Worker with over 25 years of experience in the field of social work, **I have spent my career watching the impact anxiety has on individual family members and their ability to communicate their feelings appropriately.**

As a therapist, I recognize that both anxious teens and adults find it difficult to identify their emotions correctly, and to acknowledge where emotions are felt inside their body. **When we feel anxiety, we instinctively do everything in our power to run from those emotions.** We stay busy so we don't have to feel. The thought of stillness can even terrify an anxious person because then they'd have to sit still with all their feelings. Yet our emotions eventually come out in some form. **Unfortunately, we often explode or blame others when we feel out of control or unable to express ourselves clearly.**

As a once anxious teen, now therapist, and mother who has raised three teens to adulthood, I have personally walked through the challenging parent-teen years from both sides. Today my adult children and I often talk about how helpful a tool like this would have been to communicate about the hard stuff, rather than avoid emotionally difficult conversations.

There's nothing more important than a parent-teenager bond. This journal helps you deepen that, and through this process you both will learn skills that will uplift every area of your life.

Note from the Author

Dear Reader,

I've been a Licensed Clinical Social Worker for over two decades and have spent the past 25 years of my career helping individuals and families learn to adapt and cope with difficult life transitions.

I am the creator of Combating Teen Anxiety, a proven 10-step method to reduce anxiety and give teens the skills to manage their emotions so that they can succeed in their present and future goals. I created this parent and teen communication journal to give teens the language and tools to express themselves with their parents when conversations are difficult to discuss in person.

In addition to this journal and working with people in my private practice through online training programs, virtual coaching nationwide, and in-person and online psychotherapy in California and Idaho, I offer corporate workshops and keynote speaking. My expertise is in teaching teens and adults to catch their anxiety before it gets out of control, and to practice owning, speaking, and releasing their emotions in a more productive way.

As a Certified EMDR Therapist, my specialized training helps decrease the client's negative beliefs that fuel their anxiety and provide them with a new perspective. My experience as a Certified Daring Way Facilitator™ encourages clients to embrace vulnerability as a necessary step for shame resilience and connection.

My clinical expertise combined with my personal journey raising three kids through their own challenges, and my son's gender transition, are what really helps me connect on a deeper level and transform the lives of my clients. When I'm not helping others, I love adventuring in the great outdoors with family and friends.

I hope this journal deepens your connection and brings you more joy!

—Gina Nelson, LCSW

How It Works

The journal consists of prompts that allow the **teen or parent to initiate a discussion using the fill-in-the-blank and free form response to express their feelings in a clear and productive manner**. It also helps them to articulate **what makes them feel unsafe coming to a parent or teen with concerns**. The parent or teen can then respond using the same prompts and language format.

The goal is to **pay attention to the nervous system and learn to sit with uncomfortable feelings in order to move through them, rather than run from them**. The journal is designed to allow teens and parents to slow down their thoughts, identify their emotions, and understand where they are feeling these emotions inside their body so they can better articulate their thoughts and express their needs.

It is always best to use the journal as a guide to open a deeper conversation and then discuss the situation in person. **However, if the only communication that feels safe is via the journal entry and response, that's still a big win!**

I suggest that you and your teen have a designated confidential spot (where other family members can't view) to place the journal when an entry has been initiated by either of you. You may even want to send a text notifying the other that an entry has been placed.

As a special gift to support you and your teen in this process, you might enjoy my free video training series with therapist-proven methods to help parents manage teen anxiety and catch it before it gets out of control. Just go to **www.CombatingTeenAnxiety.com** to download the free course.

I can't wait to hear how you and your teen integrate this journal into your lives, and how it helps your relationship!

Best Wishes,
Gina Nelson

Rules for Engagement Contract

1. **Use the journal after taking a moment to ground yourself emotionally.**
   Take a walk, breathe, journal, talk to a friend, cuddle with a pet, listen to calming music, etc.

2. **Assume people don't want to deliberately harm you.**
   Give each other the benefit of the doubt and assume that the other person did not intentionally try to harm you or hurt you by what they said or did.

3. **Use the positive statement first.**
   Start each sentence by acknowledging something good in the other person before expressing the thing that made you feel upset.

   i.e. *"I appreciate that you are taking the time and are concerned about me, and I sometimes feel that you are still distracted and not really hearing me."*

4. **Use "I Statements" to express your emotions instead of "You."**
   When we start a difficult conversation with "I" instead of "You", we reduce defensiveness in the other person by owning our feelings rather than blaming them for their actions.

   i.e *"I feel frustrated because…"* or *"I get triggered when…"*

5. **Avoid words that overgeneralize like *always* and *never*.**
   Words like *always* and *never* can shut down the conversation and prevent open discussion.

6. **Avoid the word *but* as it erases everything you said before it, including an apology.**
   Instead of this: *"I apologize for yelling or calling you that name, but I'm just really frustrated."*

   Use this: *"I apologize for yelling or calling you that name, and I'm just really frustrated. When I'm frustrated, I sometimes say things I don't mean."*

   This doesn't negate the apology–and it also explains the emotions behind what was said.

_____

Teen Signature

_____

Parent Signature

The Purpose of the Journal Prompts

1. **Use the journal prompt to help you find words that express your feelings.**
   Since it can often be difficult to identify the correct word to match our feelings, a feeling word choice list is provided on page 6 to support you.

2. **Use the journal prompt to help you acknowledge where you feel the emotions inside your body.**
   It's very common to not know where we feel emotions in our body, but if we can catch it in our body first, we can change our thoughts. A Body Emotion Connection Diagram is provided on page 9 to help you make the connections.

3. **Use the journal prompts to help you identify the assumptions you make, or the "story you tell yourself."**
   We all make up stories. Often we fill in the blanks with our own assumptions instead of asking for clarification.

   i.e. My son storms out of the room and slams the door in the middle of my sentence. I make up a story that he's *"disrespectful, angry at me, and that I've failed as a parent because he won't listen to me."*

4. **Circle back into conversation to get clear on your assumptions.**
   This is the most difficult step–and usually the one most people avoid–because it's easier to just move on and not "circle back" to the conversation because we fear bringing tension back up.

   Continuing with the example above in #3, when I circle back with my son, he shares that his best friend is mad at him. If I never circle back, then I would not know that it wasn't about me.

For extra help with this often challenging step, go to
www.CombatingTeenAnxiety.com for free training videos with more instruction on how to navigate this vital yet often skipped piece.

Feelings Vocabulary

Happiness	Care	Depression	Inadequate	Fear
Delighted	Compassion	Depressed	Damaged	Distressed
Excited	Kind	Devalued	Helpless	Frightened
Joyful	Empathetic	Miserable	Defeated	Terrified
Lively	Sympathetic	Melancholy	Ineffective	Intimidated
Thrilled	Friendly	Dismal	Incomplete	Afraid
Ecstatic	Thoughtful	Hopeless	Worthless	Anxious
Vibrant	Appreciative	Helpless	Insignificant	Nervous
Cheerful	Devoted	Powerless	Useless	Panicked
Content	Adoring	Discouraged	Not Enough	Uneasy
		Woeful		Worried
		Dismissed		Overwhelmed

Confusion	Hurt	Anger	Lonely	Remorse
Speechless	Abused	Irritated	Abandoned	Disgraced
Puzzled	Crushed	Infuriated	Empty	Apologetic
Bewildered	Damaged	Hostile	Isolated	Ashamed
Ambivalent	Mistreated	Resentful	Alone	Guilty
Perplexed	Let down	Furious	Forsaken	Regretful
Misled	Neglected	Enraged	Rejected	Sorrowful
Disorganized	Depreciated	Aggravated	Excluded	Remorseful
Troubled	Distressed	Grouchy	Oppressed	
	Sad	Annoyed	Outcasted	
	Ignored			
	Unseen			

Why It's Important to Connect Our Thoughts and Feelings to Our Body

Most of us don't know how to connect our emotions and thoughts to sensations inside our body. However, there is important information that our body provides to us when we are able to recognize sensations in our body as they occur.

1. **Our nervous system is designed to alert us to danger to protect us from harm** by secreting cortisol and adrenaline throughout the body so we can fight or get away (also called **"fight or flight"**).

2. Unfortunately, **our nervous system doesn't know the difference between a "real physical threat" or a "perceived threat"** so our body responds to perceived or assumed emotional threat the same way it responds to a physical threat.

3. The effects of these hormones cause **stimulating effects** such as increased heart rate, increased blood flow, increased blood pressure, increased strength, increased sweating, hair standing up, and even an increase in body temperature.

4. When we get activated by something someone said or did, **our body feels something immediately**, even before our brain articulates words.

5. The **ability to recognize and learn to identify sensations within the body** as they happen **gives us insight** that we have been emotionally triggered.

6. Our success in learning to communicate starts by **first identifying the physical response** our body feels, and then **learning to calm ourselves down before speaking**.

Free Video Training Series Download:

To give you extra support for creating a consistent practice for the both of you to use this journal.

www.CombatingTeenAnxiety.com

3-Part Video training resource
that includes PDFs, handouts,
and Therapist-Proven Methods
To Help Teen Anxiety

**Get instant access today:
www.CombatingTeenAnxiety.com**

"In working with Gina, I have progressed in many different ways. I have learned how to recognize and reduce my anxiety and respond in a way that significantly helps me."
- Emery H. (teen)

"I never would have thought I needed therapy tools, but through Gina's practice I was able to recognize why I had negative thoughts and where they were stemming from! Now I can easily say that Gina has shown me how to care for myself in ways I never knew I needed."
- Katelyn F. (college student)

"I went to Gina to deal with my anxiety and it has changed my life. One of the best decisions I've ever made. Gina is kind, empathetic and an incredible guide through difficult emotional terrain."
- Mike M.

Where Sensations or Emotions Are Held Inside Our Body

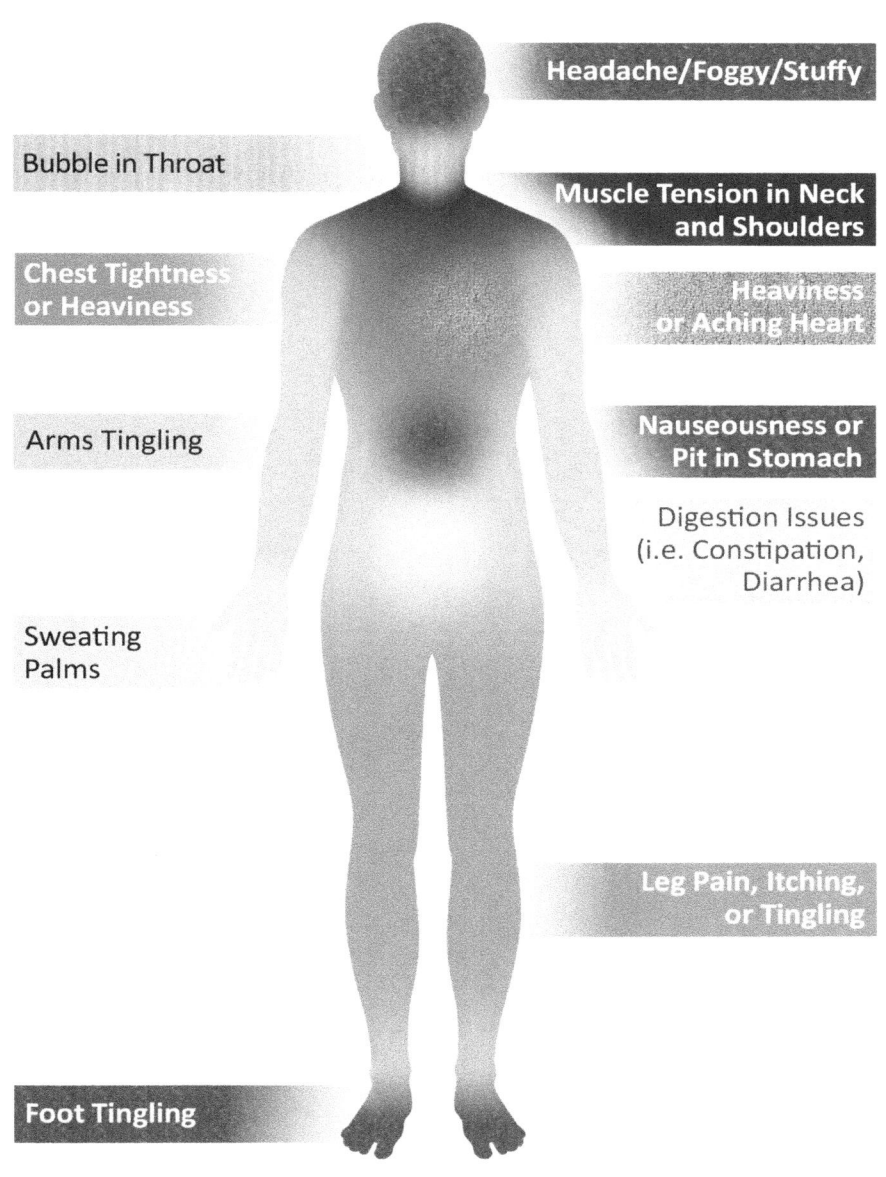

Here is an example of some of the most common sensations found in different parts of the body that can be used as emotion awareness indicators.

The Journaling Begins Now!

The rest of this journal consists of 120 empty pages with prompts to guide you and your teen on a journey of deeper connection and communication. You may use these at your discretion.

Enjoy this profound process!

Date: _____ Teen Entry

I trust that it wasn't your intention to:
_____
_____

I feel _____ when:
    {emotion(s)}
_____
_____
_____

When I'm _____, my body feels_____
        {emotion(s)}   {sensation(s)}
in my _____.
      {body part(s)}

I feel **emotionally unsafe** to talk with you when:
_____
_____

I'd feel **safer** to talk if:
_____
_____

Our relationship is important to me and:
_____
_____

Date: Parent Entry

I trust that it wasn't your intention to:
_____
_____

I feel _____ when:
      {emotion(s)}
_____
_____
_____

When I'm _____, my body feels_____
      {emotion(s)}   {sensation(s)}

in my _____.
      {body part(s)}

I feel **emotionally unsafe** to talk with you when:
_____
_____

I'd feel **safer** to talk if:
_____
_____

Our relationship is important to me and:
_____
_____

Date: _____   Teen Entry

I trust that it wasn't your intention to:
_____
_____

I feel _____ when:
       {emotion(s)}
_____
_____
_____

When I'm _____, my body feels_____
           {emotion(s)}   {sensation(s)}

in my _____.
       {body part(s)}

I feel **emotionally unsafe** to talk with you when:
_____
_____

I'd feel **safer** to talk if:
_____
_____

Our relationship is important to me and:
_____
_____

Date: _____   Parent Entry

I trust that it wasn't your intention to:
_____
_____

I feel _____ when:
      {emotion(s)}
_____
_____
_____

When I'm _____, my body feels_____
             {emotion(s)}   {sensation(s)}

in my _____.
        {body part(s)}

I feel **emotionally unsafe** to talk with you when:
_____
_____

I'd feel **safer** to talk if:
_____
_____

Our relationship is important to me and:
_____
_____

Date: Teen Entry

I trust that it wasn't your intention to:
_____
_____

I feel _____ when:
       {emotion(s)}

_____
_____
_____

When I'm _____, my body feels_____
           {emotion(s)}   {sensation(s)}

in my _____.
       {body part(s)}

I feel **emotionally unsafe** to talk with you when:
_____
_____

I'd feel **safer** to talk if:
_____
_____

Our relationship is important to me and:
_____
_____

Date: _____   Parent Entry

I trust that it wasn't your intention to:
_____
_____

I feel _____ when:
      {emotion(s)}
_____
_____
_____

When I'm _____, my body feels_____
      {emotion(s)}   {sensation(s)}

in my _____.
      {body part(s)}

I feel **emotionally unsafe** to talk with you when:
_____
_____

I'd feel **safer** to talk if:
_____
_____

Our relationship is important to me and:
_____
_____

Date: _____   Teen Entry

I trust that it wasn't your intention to:
_____
_____

I feel _____ when:
      {emotion(s)}

_____
_____
_____

When I'm _____, my body feels_____
      {emotion(s)}   {sensation(s)}

in my _____.
      {body part(s)}

I feel **emotionally unsafe** to talk with you when:
_____
_____

I'd feel **safer** to talk if:
_____
_____

Our relationship is important to me and:
_____
_____

Date: _____   Parent Entry

I trust that it wasn't your intention to:
_____
_____

I feel _____ when:
     {emotion(s)}
_____
_____
_____

When I'm _____, my body feels_____
     {emotion(s)}   {sensation(s)}

in my _____.
     {body part(s)}

I feel **emotionally unsafe** to talk with you when:
_____
_____

I'd feel **safer** to talk if:
_____
_____

Our relationship is important to me and:
_____
_____

Date: _____   Teen Entry

I trust that it wasn't your intention to:
_____
_____

I feel _____ when:
          {emotion(s)}
_____
_____
_____

When I'm _____, my body feels_____
           {emotion(s)}   {sensation(s)}

in my _____.
         {body part(s)}

I feel **emotionally unsafe** to talk with you when:
_____
_____

I'd feel **safer** to talk if:
_____
_____

Our relationship is important to me and:
_____
_____

Date: Parent Entry

I trust that it wasn't your intention to:
_____
_____

I feel _____ when:
      {emotion(s)}

_____
_____
_____

When I'm _____, my body feels_____
         {emotion(s)}   {sensation(s)}

in my _____.
      {body part(s)}

I feel **emotionally unsafe** to talk with you when:
_____
_____

I'd feel **safer** to talk if:
_____
_____

Our relationship is important to me and:
_____
_____

Date: _____   Teen Entry

I trust that it wasn't your intention to:
_____
_____

I feel _____ when:
     {emotion(s)}

_____
_____
_____

When I'm _____, my body feels _____
         {emotion(s)}   {sensation(s)}

in my _____.
       {body part(s)}

I feel **emotionally unsafe** to talk with you when:
_____
_____

I'd feel **safer** to talk if:
_____
_____

Our relationship is important to me and:
_____
_____

Date: Parent Entry

I trust that it wasn't your intention to:
_____
_____

I feel _____ when:
         {emotion(s)}

_____
_____
_____

When I'm _____, my body feels _____
          {emotion(s)}   {sensation(s)}

in my _____.
        {body part(s)}

I feel **emotionally unsafe** to talk with you when:
_____
_____

I'd feel **safer** to talk if:
_____
_____

Our relationship is important to me and:
_____
_____

Date: _____   Teen Entry

I trust that it wasn't your intention to:
_____
_____

I feel _____ when:
         {emotion(s)}

_____
_____
_____

When I'm _____, my body feels_____
              {emotion(s)}   {sensation(s)}

in my _____.
         {body part(s)}

I feel **emotionally unsafe** to talk with you when:
_____
_____

I'd feel **safer** to talk if:
_____
_____

Our relationship is important to me and:
_____
_____

Date: _____   Parent Entry

I trust that it wasn't your intention to:
_____
_____

I feel _____ when:
     {emotion(s)}
_____
_____
_____

When I'm _____, my body feels_____
     {emotion(s)}   {sensation(s)}

in my _____.
     {body part(s)}

I feel **emotionally unsafe** to talk with you when:
_____
_____

I'd feel **safer** to talk if:
_____
_____

Our relationship is important to me and:
_____
_____

Date: _____   Teen Entry

I trust that it wasn't your intention to:
_____
_____

I feel _____ when:
      {emotion(s)}
_____
_____
_____

When I'm _____, my body feels_____
        {emotion(s)}   {sensation(s)}

in my _____.
      {body part(s)}

I feel **emotionally unsafe** to talk with you when:
_____
_____

I'd feel **safer** to talk if:
_____
_____

Our relationship is important to me and:
_____
_____

Date: _____   Parent Entry

I trust that it wasn't your intention to:
_____
_____

I feel _____ when:
      {emotion(s)}
_____
_____
_____

When I'm _____, my body feels_____
      {emotion(s)}   {sensation(s)}

in my _____.
      {body part(s)}

I feel **emotionally unsafe** to talk with you when:
_____
_____

I'd feel **safer** to talk if:
_____
_____

Our relationship is important to me and:
_____
_____

Date: _____   Teen Entry

I trust that it wasn't your intention to:
_____
_____

I feel _____ when:
      {emotion(s)}

_____
_____
_____

When I'm _____, my body feels_____
      {emotion(s)}   {sensation(s)}

in my _____.
    {body part(s)}

I feel **emotionally unsafe** to talk with you when:
_____
_____

I'd feel **safer** to talk if:
_____
_____

Our relationship is important to me and:
_____
_____

Date: _____   Parent Entry

I trust that it wasn't your intention to:
_____
_____

I feel _____ when:
     {emotion(s)}
_____
_____
_____

When I'm _____, my body feels_____
            {emotion(s)}   {sensation(s)}
in my _____.
        {body part(s)}

I feel **emotionally unsafe** to talk with you when:
_____
_____

I'd feel **safer** to talk if:
_____
_____

Our relationship is important to me and:
_____
_____

Date: Teen Entry

I trust that it wasn't your intention to:
_____
_____

I feel _____ when:
      {emotion(s)}

_____
_____
_____

When I'm _____, my body feels_____
      {emotion(s)}   {sensation(s)}

in my _____.
      {body part(s)}

I feel **emotionally unsafe** to talk with you when:
_____
_____

I'd feel **safer** to talk if:
_____
_____

Our relationship is important to me and:
_____
_____

Date: Parent Entry

I trust that it wasn't your intention to:
_____
_____

I feel _____ when:
      {emotion(s)}
_____
_____
_____

When I'm _____, my body feels_____
      {emotion(s)}   {sensation(s)}

in my _____.
      {body part(s)}

I feel **emotionally unsafe** to talk with you when:
_____
_____

I'd feel **safer** to talk if:
_____
_____

Our relationship is important to me and:
_____
_____

Date: _____   Teen Entry

I trust that it wasn't your intention to:
_____
_____

I feel _____ when:
      {emotion(s)}
_____
_____
_____

When I'm _____, my body feels_____
          {emotion(s)}   {sensation(s)}

in my _____.
      {body part(s)}

I feel **emotionally unsafe** to talk with you when:
_____
_____

I'd feel **safer** to talk if:
_____
_____

Our relationship is important to me and:
_____
_____

Date: Parent Entry

I trust that it wasn't your intention to:
_____
_____

I feel _____ when:
      {emotion(s)}

_____
_____

When I'm _____, my body feels_____
         {emotion(s)}   {sensation(s)}

in my _____.
        {body part(s)}

I feel **emotionally unsafe** to talk with you when:
_____
_____

I'd feel **safer** to talk if:
_____
_____

Our relationship is important to me and:
_____
_____

Date: Teen Entry

I trust that it wasn't your intention to:
_____
_____

I feel _____ when:
      {emotion(s)}

_____
_____
_____

When I'm _____, my body feels_____
      {emotion(s)}   {sensation(s)}

in my _____.
      {body part(s)}

I feel **emotionally unsafe** to talk with you when:
_____
_____

I'd feel **safer** to talk if:
_____
_____

Our relationship is important to me and:
_____
_____

Date: Parent Entry

I trust that it wasn't your intention to:
_____
_____

I feel _____ when:
       {emotion(s)}
_____
_____
_____

When I'm _____, my body feels_____
           {emotion(s)}   {sensation(s)}
in my _____.
       {body part(s)}

I feel **emotionally unsafe** to talk with you when:
_____
_____

I'd feel **safer** to talk if:
_____
_____

Our relationship is important to me and:
_____
_____

Date: _____   Teen Entry

I trust that it wasn't your intention to:
_____
_____

I feel _____ when:
      {emotion(s)}
_____
_____
_____

When I'm _____, my body feels_____
      {emotion(s)}   {sensation(s)}

in my _____.
    {body part(s)}

I feel **emotionally unsafe** to talk with you when:
_____
_____

I'd feel **safer** to talk if:
_____
_____

Our relationship is important to me and:
_____
_____

Date: Parent Entry

I trust that it wasn't your intention to:
_____
_____

I feel _____ when:
       {emotion(s)}
_____
_____
_____

When I'm _____, my body feels_____
              {emotion(s)}   {sensation(s)}

in my _____.
         {body part(s)}

I feel **emotionally unsafe** to talk with you when:
_____
_____

I'd feel **safer** to talk if:
_____
_____

Our relationship is important to me and:
_____
_____

Date: _____   Teen Entry

I trust that it wasn't your intention to:
_____
_____

I feel _____ when:
      {emotion(s)}

_____
_____
_____

When I'm _____, my body feels_____
      {emotion(s)}   {sensation(s)}

in my _____.
      {body part(s)}

I feel **emotionally unsafe** to talk with you when:
_____
_____

I'd feel **safer** to talk if:
_____
_____

Our relationship is important to me and:
_____
_____

Date: _____   Parent Entry

I trust that it wasn't your intention to:
_____
_____

I feel _____ when:
     {emotion(s)}

_____
_____
_____

When I'm _____, my body feels_____
     {emotion(s)}   {sensation(s)}

in my _____.
     {body part(s)}

I feel **emotionally unsafe** to talk with you when:
_____
_____

I'd feel **safer** to talk if:
_____
_____

Our relationship is important to me and:
_____
_____

Date: Teen Entry

I trust that it wasn't your intention to:

_____

_____

I feel _____ when:
          {emotion(s)}

_____

_____

_____

When I'm _____, my body feels_____
               {emotion(s)}   {sensation(s)}

in my _____.
          {body part(s)}

I feel **emotionally unsafe** to talk with you when:

_____

_____

I'd feel **safer** to talk if:

_____

_____

Our relationship is important to me and:

_____

_____

Date: Parent Entry

I trust that it wasn't your intention to:
_____
_____

I feel _____ when:
      {emotion(s)}

_____
_____
_____

When I'm _____, my body feels_____
      {emotion(s)}   {sensation(s)}

in my _____.
      {body part(s)}

I feel **emotionally unsafe** to talk with you when:
_____
_____

I'd feel **safer** to talk if:
_____
_____

Our relationship is important to me and:
_____
_____

Date: _____   Teen Entry

I trust that it wasn't your intention to:
_____
_____

I feel _____ when:
      {emotion(s)}

_____
_____
_____

When I'm _____, my body feels_____
          {emotion(s)}   {sensation(s)}

in my _____.
        {body part(s)}

I feel **emotionally unsafe** to talk with you when:
_____
_____

I'd feel **safer** to talk if:
_____
_____

Our relationship is important to me and:
_____
_____

Date: _____   Parent Entry

I trust that it wasn't your intention to:
_____
_____

I feel _____ when:
      {emotion(s)}
_____
_____
_____

When I'm _____, my body feels_____
              {emotion(s)}   {sensation(s)}

in my _____.
         {body part(s)}

I feel **emotionally unsafe** to talk with you when:
_____
_____

I'd feel **safer** to talk if:
_____
_____

Our relationship is important to me and:
_____
_____

Date: Teen Entry

I trust that it wasn't your intention to:
_____
_____

I feel _____ when:
        {emotion(s)}
_____
_____
_____

When I'm _____, my body feels_____
            {emotion(s)}   {sensation(s)}

in my _____.
        {body part(s)}

I feel **emotionally unsafe** to talk with you when:
_____
_____

I'd feel **safer** to talk if:
_____
_____

Our relationship is important to me and:
_____
_____

Date: Parent Entry

I trust that it wasn't your intention to:
_____
_____

I feel _____ when:
      {emotion(s)}

_____
_____

When I'm _____, my body feels_____
      {emotion(s)}   {sensation(s)}

in my _____.
      {body part(s)}

I feel **emotionally unsafe** to talk with you when:
_____
_____

I'd feel **safer** to talk if:
_____
_____

Our relationship is important to me and:
_____
_____

Date: _____   Teen Entry

I trust that it wasn't your intention to:
_____
_____

I feel _____ when:
      {emotion(s)}

_____
_____
_____

When I'm _____, my body feels_____
         {emotion(s)}   {sensation(s)}

in my _____.
        {body part(s)}

I feel **emotionally unsafe** to talk with you when:
_____
_____

I'd feel **safer** to talk if:
_____
_____

Our relationship is important to me and:
_____
_____

Date: Parent Entry

I trust that it wasn't your intention to:
_____
_____

I feel _____ when:
    {emotion(s)}

_____
_____

When I'm _____, my body feels_____
    {emotion(s)}   {sensation(s)}

in my _____.
    {body part(s)}

I feel **emotionally unsafe** to talk with you when:
_____
_____

I'd feel **safer** to talk if:
_____
_____

Our relationship is important to me and:
_____
_____

Date: Teen Entry

I trust that it wasn't your intention to:

_____

_____

I feel _____ when:
       {emotion(s)}

_____

_____

_____

When I'm _____, my body feels _____
                 {emotion(s)}   {sensation(s)}

in my _____.
          {body part(s)}

I feel **emotionally unsafe** to talk with you when:

_____

_____

I'd feel **safer** to talk if:

_____

_____

Our relationship is important to me and:

_____

_____

Date: _____   Parent Entry

I trust that it wasn't your intention to:
_____
_____

I feel _____ when:
         {emotion(s)}
_____
_____
_____

When I'm _____, my body feels _____
              {emotion(s)}   {sensation(s)}

in my _____.
         {body part(s)}

I feel **emotionally unsafe** to talk with you when:
_____
_____

I'd feel **safer** to talk if:
_____
_____

Our relationship is important to me and:
_____
_____

Date: Teen Entry

I trust that it wasn't your intention to:
_____
_____

I feel _____ when:
     {emotion(s)}

_____
_____
_____

When I'm _____, my body feels_____
         {emotion(s)}   {sensation(s)}

in my _____.
         {body part(s)}

I feel **emotionally unsafe** to talk with you when:
_____
_____

I'd feel **safer** to talk if:
_____
_____

Our relationship is important to me and:
_____
_____

Date: Parent Entry

I trust that it wasn't your intention to:
_____
_____

I feel _____ when:
           {emotion(s)}
_____
_____
_____

When I'm _____, my body feels_____
              {emotion(s)}   {sensation(s)}
in my _____.
          {body part(s)}

I feel **emotionally unsafe** to talk with you when:
_____
_____

I'd feel **safer** to talk if:
_____
_____

Our relationship is important to me and:
_____
_____

Date: _____ Teen Entry

I trust that it wasn't your intention to:
_____
_____

I feel _____ when:
      {emotion(s)}
_____
_____
_____

When I'm _____, my body feels_____
      {emotion(s)}   {sensation(s)}

in my _____.
      {body part(s)}

I feel **emotionally unsafe** to talk with you when:
_____
_____

I'd feel **safer** to talk if:
_____
_____

Our relationship is important to me and:
_____
_____

Date: _____   Parent Entry

I trust that it wasn't your intention to:
_____
_____

I feel _____ when:
       {emotion(s)}

_____
_____
_____

When I'm _____, my body feels_____
              {emotion(s)}   {sensation(s)}

in my _____.
        {body part(s)}

I feel **emotionally unsafe** to talk with you when:
_____
_____

I'd feel **safer** to talk if:
_____
_____

Our relationship is important to me and:
_____
_____

Date: _____ Teen Entry

I trust that it wasn't your intention to:
_____
_____

I feel _____ when:
     {emotion(s)}

_____
_____
_____

When I'm _____, my body feels_____
          {emotion(s)}   {sensation(s)}

in my _____.
     {body part(s)}

I feel **emotionally unsafe** to talk with you when:
_____
_____

I'd feel **safer** to talk if:
_____
_____

Our relationship is important to me and:
_____
_____

Date: Parent Entry

I trust that it wasn't your intention to:
_____
_____

I feel _____ when:
      {emotion(s)}
_____
_____
_____

When I'm _____, my body feels_____
      {emotion(s)}   {sensation(s)}

in my _____.
      {body part(s)}

I feel **emotionally unsafe** to talk with you when:
_____
_____

I'd feel **safer** to talk if:
_____
_____

Our relationship is important to me and:
_____
_____

Date: Teen Entry

I trust that it wasn't your intention to:
_____
_____

I feel _____ when:
       {emotion(s)}

_____
_____
_____

When I'm _____, my body feels_____
              {emotion(s)}   {sensation(s)}

in my _____.
             {body part(s)}

I feel **emotionally unsafe** to talk with you when:
_____
_____

I'd feel **safer** to talk if:
_____
_____

Our relationship is important to me and:
_____
_____

Date: _____ Parent Entry

I trust that it wasn't your intention to:
_____
_____

I feel _____ when:
      {emotion(s)}
_____
_____
_____

When I'm _____, my body feels_____
            {emotion(s)}   {sensation(s)}

in my _____.
      {body part(s)}

I feel **emotionally unsafe** to talk with you when:
_____
_____

I'd feel **safer** to talk if:
_____
_____

Our relationship is important to me and:
_____
_____

Date: Teen Entry

I trust that it wasn't your intention to:

_____

_____

I feel _____ when:
        {emotion(s)}

_____

_____

_____

When I'm _____, my body feels_____
             {emotion(s)}   {sensation(s)}

in my _____.
          {body part(s)}

I feel **emotionally unsafe** to talk with you when:

_____

_____

I'd feel **safer** to talk if:

_____

_____

Our relationship is important to me and:

_____

_____

Date: Parent Entry

I trust that it wasn't your intention to:

_____

_____

I feel _____ when:
       {emotion(s)}

_____

_____

When I'm _____, my body feels_____
            {emotion(s)}   {sensation(s)}

in my _____.
          {body part(s)}

I feel **emotionally unsafe** to talk with you when:

_____

_____

I'd feel **safer** to talk if:

_____

_____

Our relationship is important to me and:

_____

_____

Date: _____   Teen Entry

I trust that it wasn't your intention to:
_____
_____

I feel _____ when:
      {emotion(s)}
_____
_____
_____

When I'm _____, my body feels _____
      {emotion(s)}   {sensation(s)}

in my _____.
      {body part(s)}

I feel **emotionally unsafe** to talk with you when:
_____
_____

I'd feel **safer** to talk if:
_____
_____

Our relationship is important to me and:
_____
_____

Date: Parent Entry

I trust that it wasn't your intention to:
_____
_____

I feel _____ when:
       {emotion(s)}

_____
_____
_____

When I'm _____, my body feels_____
              {emotion(s)}   {sensation(s)}

in my _____.
        {body part(s)}

I feel **emotionally unsafe** to talk with you when:
_____
_____

I'd feel **safer** to talk if:
_____
_____

Our relationship is important to me and:
_____
_____

Date: Teen Entry

I trust that it wasn't your intention to:
_____
_____

I feel _____ when:
     {emotion(s)}

_____
_____
_____

When I'm _____, my body feels_____
            {emotion(s)}   {sensation(s)}

in my _____.
         {body part(s)}

I feel **emotionally unsafe** to talk with you when:
_____
_____

I'd feel **safer** to talk if:
_____
_____

Our relationship is important to me and:
_____
_____

Date: _____   Parent Entry

I trust that it wasn't your intention to:
_____
_____

I feel _____ when:
       {emotion(s)}
_____
_____
_____

When I'm _____, my body feels_____
             {emotion(s)}   {sensation(s)}

in my _____.
       {body part(s)}

I feel **emotionally unsafe** to talk with you when:
_____
_____

I'd feel **safer** to talk if:
_____
_____

Our relationship is important to me and:
_____
_____

Date: _____   Teen Entry

I trust that it wasn't your intention to:
_____
_____

I feel _____ when:
      {emotion(s)}

_____
_____
_____

When I'm _____, my body feels_____
      {emotion(s)}   {sensation(s)}

in my _____.
      {body part(s)}

I feel **emotionally unsafe** to talk with you when:
_____
_____

I'd feel **safer** to talk if:
_____
_____

Our relationship is important to me and:
_____
_____

Date: Parent Entry

I trust that it wasn't your intention to:
_____
_____

I feel _____ when:
      {emotion(s)}
_____
_____
_____

When I'm _____, my body feels_____
          {emotion(s)}   {sensation(s)}

in my _____.
      {body part(s)}

I feel **emotionally unsafe** to talk with you when:
_____
_____

I'd feel **safer** to talk if:
_____
_____

Our relationship is important to me and:
_____
_____

Date: _____ Teen Entry

I trust that it wasn't your intention to:
_____
_____

I feel _____ when:
      {emotion(s)}

_____
_____
_____

When I'm _____, my body feels_____
            {emotion(s)}   {sensation(s)}

in my _____.
          {body part(s)}

I feel **emotionally unsafe** to talk with you when:
_____
_____

I'd feel **safer** to talk if:
_____
_____

Our relationship is important to me and:
_____
_____

Date: Parent Entry

I trust that it wasn't your intention to:
_____
_____

I feel _____ when:
         {emotion(s)}

_____

_____

When I'm _____, my body feels_____
              {emotion(s)}   {sensation(s)}

in my _____.
         {body part(s)}

I feel **emotionally unsafe** to talk with you when:
_____
_____

I'd feel **safer** to talk if:
_____
_____

Our relationship is important to me and:
_____
_____

Date: _____   Teen Entry

I trust that it wasn't your intention to:
_____
_____

I feel _____ when:
      {emotion(s)}

_____
_____
_____

When I'm _____, my body feels_____
            {emotion(s)}   {sensation(s)}

in my _____.
        {body part(s)}

I feel **emotionally unsafe** to talk with you when:
_____
_____

I'd feel **safer** to talk if:
_____
_____

Our relationship is important to me and:
_____
_____

Date: _____   Parent Entry

I trust that it wasn't your intention to:
_____
_____

I feel _____ when:
      {emotion(s)}
_____
_____
_____

When I'm _____, my body feels_____
        {emotion(s)}   {sensation(s)}

in my _____.
      {body part(s)}

I feel **emotionally unsafe** to talk with you when:
_____
_____

I'd feel **safer** to talk if:
_____
_____

Our relationship is important to me and:
_____
_____

Date: Teen Entry

I trust that it wasn't your intention to:
_____
_____

I feel _____ when:
      {emotion(s)}

_____
_____
_____

When I'm _____, my body feels_____
      {emotion(s)}   {sensation(s)}

in my _____.
      {body part(s)}

I feel **emotionally unsafe** to talk with you when:
_____
_____

I'd feel **safer** to talk if:
_____
_____

Our relationship is important to me and:
_____
_____

Date: Parent Entry

I trust that it wasn't your intention to:
_____
_____

I feel _____ when:
        {emotion(s)}

_____
_____
_____

When I'm _____, my body feels_____
             {emotion(s)}   {sensation(s)}

in my _____.
           {body part(s)}

I feel **emotionally unsafe** to talk with you when:
_____
_____

I'd feel **safer** to talk if:
_____
_____

Our relationship is important to me and:
_____
_____

Date: _____   Teen Entry

I trust that it wasn't your intention to:
_____
_____

I feel _____ when:
      {emotion(s)}

_____
_____
_____

When I'm _____, my body feels_____
      {emotion(s)}   {sensation(s)}

in my _____.
      {body part(s)}

I feel **emotionally unsafe** to talk with you when:
_____
_____

I'd feel **safer** to talk if:
_____
_____

Our relationship is important to me and:
_____
_____

Date: Parent Entry

I trust that it wasn't your intention to:
_____
_____

I feel _____ when:
      {emotion(s)}

_____
_____

When I'm _____, my body feels_____
          {emotion(s)}   {sensation(s)}

in my _____.
      {body part(s)}

I feel **emotionally unsafe** to talk with you when:
_____
_____

I'd feel **safer** to talk if:
_____
_____

Our relationship is important to me and:
_____
_____

Date: Teen Entry

I trust that it wasn't your intention to:

_____

_____

I feel _____ when:
        {emotion(s)}

_____

_____

_____

When I'm _____, my body feels_____
            {emotion(s)}   {sensation(s)}

in my _____.
           {body part(s)}

I feel **emotionally unsafe** to talk with you when:

_____

_____

I'd feel **safer** to talk if:

_____

_____

Our relationship is important to me and:

_____

_____

Date: Parent Entry

I trust that it wasn't your intention to:
_____
_____

I feel _____ when:
      {emotion(s)}

_____
_____

When I'm _____, my body feels _____
           {emotion(s)}   {sensation(s)}

in my _____.
         {body part(s)}

I feel **emotionally unsafe** to talk with you when:
_____
_____

I'd feel **safer** to talk if:
_____
_____

Our relationship is important to me and:
_____
_____

Date: Teen Entry

I trust that it wasn't your intention to:
_____
_____

I feel _____ when:
      {emotion(s)}

_____
_____
_____

When I'm _____, my body feels _____
            {emotion(s)}   {sensation(s)}

in my _____.
      {body part(s)}

I feel **emotionally unsafe** to talk with you when:
_____
_____

I'd feel **safer** to talk if:
_____
_____

Our relationship is important to me and:
_____
_____

Date: Parent Entry

I trust that it wasn't your intention to:

_____

_____

I feel _____ when:
       {emotion(s)}

_____

_____

_____

When I'm _____, my body feels _____
             {emotion(s)}   {sensation(s)}

in my _____.
          {body part(s)}

I feel **emotionally unsafe** to talk with you when:

_____

_____

I'd feel **safer** to talk if:

_____

_____

Our relationship is important to me and:

_____

_____

Date: Teen Entry

I trust that it wasn't your intention to:

_____

_____

I feel _____ when:
      {emotion(s)}

_____

_____

_____

When I'm _____, my body feels_____
            {emotion(s)}   {sensation(s)}

in my _____.
      {body part(s)}

I feel **emotionally unsafe** to talk with you when:

_____

_____

I'd feel **safer** to talk if:

_____

_____

Our relationship is important to me and:

_____

_____

Date: Parent Entry

I trust that it wasn't your intention to:
_____
_____

I feel _____ when:
       {emotion(s)}

_____
_____

When I'm _____, my body feels_____
              {emotion(s)}   {sensation(s)}

in my _____.
         {body part(s)}

I feel **emotionally unsafe** to talk with you when:
_____
_____

I'd feel **safer** to talk if:
_____
_____

Our relationship is important to me and:
_____
_____

Date: _____   Teen Entry

I trust that it wasn't your intention to:
_____
_____

I feel _____ when:
      {emotion(s)}
_____
_____
_____

When I'm _____, my body feels_____
         {emotion(s)}   {sensation(s)}

in my _____.
      {body part(s)}

I feel **emotionally unsafe** to talk with you when:
_____
_____

I'd feel **safer** to talk if:
_____
_____

Our relationship is important to me and:
_____
_____

Date: Parent Entry

I trust that it wasn't your intention to:
_____
_____

I feel _____ when:
      {emotion(s)}

_____
_____
_____

When I'm _____, my body feels_____
         {emotion(s)}   {sensation(s)}

in my _____.
      {body part(s)}

I feel **emotionally unsafe** to talk with you when:
_____
_____

I'd feel **safer** to talk if:
_____
_____

Our relationship is important to me and:
_____
_____

Date: _____   Teen Entry

I trust that it wasn't your intention to:
_____
_____

I feel _____ when:
     {emotion(s)}

_____
_____
_____

When I'm _____, my body feels_____
         {emotion(s)}   {sensation(s)}

in my _____.
     {body part(s)}

I feel **emotionally unsafe** to talk with you when:
_____
_____

I'd feel **safer** to talk if:
_____
_____

Our relationship is important to me and:
_____
_____

Date: Parent Entry

I trust that it wasn't your intention to:
_____
_____

I feel _____ when:
        {emotion(s)}

_____
_____
_____

When I'm _____, my body feels_____
                {emotion(s)}   {sensation(s)}

in my _____.
          {body part(s)}

I feel **emotionally unsafe** to talk with you when:
_____
_____

I'd feel **safer** to talk if:
_____
_____

Our relationship is important to me and:
_____
_____

Date: _____   Teen Entry

I trust that it wasn't your intention to:
_____
_____

I feel _____ when:
      {emotion(s)}

_____
_____
_____

When I'm _____, my body feels_____
             {emotion(s)}   {sensation(s)}

in my _____.
        {body part(s)}

I feel **emotionally unsafe** to talk with you when:
_____
_____

I'd feel **safer** to talk if:
_____
_____

Our relationship is important to me and:
_____
_____

Date: Parent Entry

I trust that it wasn't your intention to:
_____
_____

I feel _____ when:
        {emotion(s)}
_____
_____
_____

When I'm _____, my body feels_____
               {emotion(s)}   {sensation(s)}

in my _____.
           {body part(s)}

I feel **emotionally unsafe** to talk with you when:
_____
_____

I'd feel **safer** to talk if:
_____
_____

Our relationship is important to me and:
_____
_____

Date: Teen Entry

I trust that it wasn't your intention to:

_____

_____

I feel _____ when:
      {emotion(s)}

_____

_____

_____

When I'm _____, my body feels_____
          {emotion(s)}   {sensation(s)}

in my _____.
       {body part(s)}

I feel **emotionally unsafe** to talk with you when:

_____

_____

I'd feel **safer** to talk if:

_____

_____

Our relationship is important to me and:

_____

_____

Date: _____   Parent Entry

I trust that it wasn't your intention to:
_____
_____

I feel _____ when:
      {emotion(s)}

_____
_____
_____

When I'm _____, my body feels _____
        {emotion(s)}   {sensation(s)}

in my _____.
      {body part(s)}

I feel **emotionally unsafe** to talk with you when:
_____
_____

I'd feel **safer** to talk if:
_____
_____

Our relationship is important to me and:
_____
_____

Date: _____   Teen Entry

I trust that it wasn't your intention to:
_____
_____

I feel _____ when:
　　　{emotion(s)}

_____
_____
_____

When I'm _____, my body feels_____
　　　　　{emotion(s)}　　　　　　　　　　　　{sensation(s)}

in my _____.
　　　{body part(s)}

I feel **emotionally unsafe** to talk with you when:
_____
_____

I'd feel **safer** to talk if:
_____
_____

Our relationship is important to me and:
_____
_____

Date: Parent Entry

I trust that it wasn't your intention to:
_____
_____

I feel _____ when:
      {emotion(s)}
_____
_____
_____

When I'm _____, my body feels_____
           {emotion(s)}   {sensation(s)}

in my _____.
      {body part(s)}

I feel **emotionally unsafe** to talk with you when:
_____
_____

I'd feel **safer** to talk if:
_____
_____

Our relationship is important to me and:
_____
_____

Date: _____   Teen Entry

I trust that it wasn't your intention to:
_____
_____

I feel _____ when:
     {emotion(s)}

_____
_____
_____

When I'm _____, my body feels_____
          {emotion(s)}   {sensation(s)}

in my _____.
       {body part(s)}

I feel **emotionally unsafe** to talk with you when:
_____
_____

I'd feel **safer** to talk if:
_____
_____

Our relationship is important to me and:
_____
_____

Date: _____   Parent Entry

I trust that it wasn't your intention to:
_____
_____

I feel _____ when:
      {emotion(s)}

_____
_____
_____

When I'm _____, my body feels_____
      {emotion(s)}   {sensation(s)}

in my _____.
      {body part(s)}

I feel **emotionally unsafe** to talk with you when:
_____
_____

I'd feel **safer** to talk if:
_____
_____

Our relationship is important to me and:
_____
_____

Date: _____ Teen Entry

I trust that it wasn't your intention to:
_____
_____

I feel _____ when:
      {emotion(s)}

_____
_____

When I'm _____, my body feels _____
            {emotion(s)}   {sensation(s)}

in my _____.
        {body part(s)}

I feel **emotionally unsafe** to talk with you when:
_____
_____

I'd feel **safer** to talk if:
_____
_____

Our relationship is important to me and:
_____
_____

Date: Parent Entry

I trust that it wasn't your intention to:
_____
_____

I feel _____ when:
         {emotion(s)}
_____
_____
_____

When I'm _____, my body feels_____
              {emotion(s)}   {sensation(s)}
in my _____.
         {body part(s)}

I feel **emotionally unsafe** to talk with you when:
_____
_____

I'd feel **safer** to talk if:
_____
_____

Our relationship is important to me and:
_____
_____

Date: _____ Teen Entry

I trust that it wasn't your intention to:
_____
_____

I feel _____ when:
     {emotion(s)}

_____
_____
_____

When I'm _____, my body feels_____
        {emotion(s)}   {sensation(s)}

in my _____.
        {body part(s)}

I feel **emotionally unsafe** to talk with you when:
_____
_____

I'd feel **safer** to talk if:
_____
_____

Our relationship is important to me and:
_____
_____

Date: Parent Entry

I trust that it wasn't your intention to:
_____
_____

I feel _____ when:
      {emotion(s)}

_____
_____

When I'm _____, my body feels_____
          {emotion(s)}   {sensation(s)}

in my _____.
      {body part(s)}

I feel **emotionally unsafe** to talk with you when:
_____
_____

I'd feel **safer** to talk if:
_____
_____

Our relationship is important to me and:
_____
_____

Date: Teen Entry

I trust that it wasn't your intention to:
_____
_____

I feel _____ when:
      {emotion(s)}

_____
_____
_____

When I'm _____, my body feels_____
             {emotion(s)}   {sensation(s)}

in my _____.
      {body part(s)}

I feel **emotionally unsafe** to talk with you when:
_____
_____

I'd feel **safer** to talk if:
_____
_____

Our relationship is important to me and:
_____
_____

Date: Parent Entry

I trust that it wasn't your intention to:
_____
_____

I feel _____ when:
      {emotion(s)}
_____
_____
_____

When I'm _____, my body feels _____
      {emotion(s)}   {sensation(s)}

in my _____.
      {body part(s)}

I feel **emotionally unsafe** to talk with you when:
_____
_____

I'd feel **safer** to talk if:
_____
_____

Our relationship is important to me and:
_____
_____

Date: _____   Teen Entry

I trust that it wasn't your intention to:
_____
_____

I feel _____ when:
     {emotion(s)}

_____
_____
_____

When I'm _____, my body feels_____
     {emotion(s)}   {sensation(s)}

in my _____.
     {body part(s)}

I feel **emotionally unsafe** to talk with you when:
_____
_____

I'd feel **safer** to talk if:
_____
_____

Our relationship is important to me and:
_____
_____

Date: Parent Entry

I trust that it wasn't your intention to:
_____
_____

I feel _____ when:
      {emotion(s)}

_____
_____
_____

When I'm _____, my body feels_____
      {emotion(s)}   {sensation(s)}

in my _____.
      {body part(s)}

I feel **emotionally unsafe** to talk with you when:
_____
_____

I'd feel **safer** to talk if:
_____
_____

Our relationship is important to me and:
_____
_____

Date: _____ Teen Entry

I trust that it wasn't your intention to:
_____
_____

I feel _____ when:
   {emotion(s)}
_____
_____
_____

When I'm _____, my body feels_____
         {emotion(s)}   {sensation(s)}

in my _____.
         {body part(s)}

I feel **emotionally unsafe** to talk with you when:
_____
_____

I'd feel **safer** to talk if:
_____
_____

Our relationship is important to me and:
_____
_____

Date: Parent Entry

I trust that it wasn't your intention to:
_____
_____

I feel _____ when:
       {emotion(s)}
_____
_____

When I'm _____, my body feels _____
           {emotion(s)}   {sensation(s)}
in my _____.
          {body part(s)}

I feel **emotionally unsafe** to talk with you when:
_____
_____

I'd feel **safer** to talk if:
_____
_____

Our relationship is important to me and:
_____
_____

Date: Teen Entry

I trust that it wasn't your intention to:
_____
_____

I feel _____ when:
            {emotion(s)}

_____
_____
_____

When I'm _____, my body feels_____
            {emotion(s)}   {sensation(s)}

in my _____.
            {body part(s)}

I feel **emotionally unsafe** to talk with you when:
_____
_____

I'd feel **safer** to talk if:
_____
_____

Our relationship is important to me and:
_____
_____

Date: Parent Entry

I trust that it wasn't your intention to:
_____
_____

I feel _____ when:
       {emotion(s)}

_____
_____
_____

When I'm _____, my body feels_____
            {emotion(s)}   {sensation(s)}

in my _____.
        {body part(s)}

I feel **emotionally unsafe** to talk with you when:
_____
_____

I'd feel **safer** to talk if:
_____
_____

Our relationship is important to me and:
_____
_____

Date: _____   Teen Entry

I trust that it wasn't your intention to:
_____
_____

I feel _____ when:
        {emotion(s)}
_____
_____
_____

When I'm _____, my body feels_____
           {emotion(s)}   {sensation(s)}

in my _____.
       {body part(s)}

I feel **emotionally unsafe** to talk with you when:
_____
_____

I'd feel **safer** to talk if:
_____
_____

Our relationship is important to me and:
_____
_____

Date: Parent Entry

I trust that it wasn't your intention to:
_____
_____

I feel _____ when:
      {emotion(s)}
_____
_____
_____

When I'm _____, my body feels_____
           {emotion(s)}   {sensation(s)}

in my _____.
          {body part(s)}

I feel **emotionally unsafe** to talk with you when:
_____
_____

I'd feel **safer** to talk if:
_____
_____

Our relationship is important to me and:
_____
_____

Date: _____   Teen Entry

I trust that it wasn't your intention to:
_____
_____

I feel _____ when:
      {emotion(s)}

_____
_____
_____

When I'm _____, my body feels_____
      {emotion(s)}   {sensation(s)}

in my _____.
      {body part(s)}

I feel **emotionally unsafe** to talk with you when:
_____
_____

I'd feel **safer** to talk if:
_____
_____

Our relationship is important to me and:
_____
_____

Date: Parent Entry

I trust that it wasn't your intention to:
_____
_____

I feel _____ when:
      {emotion(s)}

_____
_____

When I'm _____, my body feels_____
      {emotion(s)}   {sensation(s)}

in my _____.
      {body part(s)}

I feel **emotionally unsafe** to talk with you when:
_____
_____

I'd feel **safer** to talk if:
_____
_____

Our relationship is important to me and:
_____
_____

Date: Teen Entry

I trust that it wasn't your intention to:
_____
_____

I feel _____ when:
      {emotion(s)}

_____
_____
_____

When I'm _____, my body feels_____
      {emotion(s)}   {sensation(s)}

in my _____.
    {body part(s)}

I feel **emotionally unsafe** to talk with you when:
_____
_____

I'd feel **safer** to talk if:
_____
_____

Our relationship is important to me and:
_____
_____

Date: _____   Parent Entry

I trust that it wasn't your intention to:
_____
_____

I feel _____ when:
       {emotion(s)}
_____
_____
_____

When I'm _____, my body feels_____
            {emotion(s)}   {sensation(s)}
in my _____.
         {body part(s)}

I feel **emotionally unsafe** to talk with you when:
_____
_____

I'd feel **safer** to talk if:
_____
_____

Our relationship is important to me and:
_____
_____

Date: _____   Teen Entry

I trust that it wasn't your intention to:
_____
_____

I feel _____ when:
      {emotion(s)}

_____
_____
_____

When I'm _____, my body feels _____
          {emotion(s)}   {sensation(s)}

in my _____.
      {body part(s)}

I feel **emotionally unsafe** to talk with you when:
_____
_____

I'd feel **safer** to talk if:
_____
_____

Our relationship is important to me and:
_____
_____

Date: _____   Parent Entry

I trust that it wasn't your intention to:
_____
_____

I feel _____ when:
    {emotion(s)}

_____
_____
_____

When I'm _____, my body feels_____
    {emotion(s)}   {sensation(s)}

in my _____.
    {body part(s)}

I feel **emotionally unsafe** to talk with you when:
_____
_____

I'd feel **safer** to talk if:
_____
_____

Our relationship is important to me and:
_____
_____

Date: _____ Teen Entry

I trust that it wasn't your intention to:
_____
_____

I feel _____ when:
      {emotion(s)}
_____
_____
_____

When I'm _____, my body feels_____
      {emotion(s)}   {sensation(s)}

in my _____.
      {body part(s)}

I feel **emotionally unsafe** to talk with you when:
_____
_____

I'd feel **safer** to talk if:
_____
_____

Our relationship is important to me and:
_____
_____

Date: Parent Entry

I trust that it wasn't your intention to:
_____
_____

I feel _____ when:
      {emotion(s)}
_____
_____
_____

When I'm _____, my body feels_____
         {emotion(s)}   {sensation(s)}
in my _____.
      {body part(s)}

I feel **emotionally unsafe** to talk with you when:
_____
_____

I'd feel **safer** to talk if:
_____
_____

Our relationship is important to me and:
_____
_____

Date: _____   Teen Entry

I trust that it wasn't your intention to:
_____
_____

I feel _____ when:
      {emotion(s)}
_____
_____
_____

When I'm _____, my body feels_____
      {emotion(s)}   {sensation(s)}

in my _____.
      {body part(s)}

I feel **emotionally unsafe** to talk with you when:
_____
_____

I'd feel **safer** to talk if:
_____
_____

Our relationship is important to me and:
_____
_____

Date: _____ Parent Entry

I trust that it wasn't your intention to:
_____
_____

I feel _____ when:
      {emotion(s)}
_____
_____
_____

When I'm _____, my body feels _____
      {emotion(s)}   {sensation(s)}

in my _____.
      {body part(s)}

I feel **emotionally unsafe** to talk with you when:
_____
_____

I'd feel **safer** to talk if:
_____
_____

Our relationship is important to me and:
_____
_____

Date: Teen Entry

I trust that it wasn't your intention to:

_____

_____

I feel _____ when:
       {emotion(s)}

_____

_____

_____

When I'm _____, my body feels_____
             {emotion(s)}   {sensation(s)}

in my _____.
          {body part(s)}

I feel **emotionally unsafe** to talk with you when:

_____

_____

I'd feel **safer** to talk if:

_____

_____

Our relationship is important to me and:

_____

_____

Date: Parent Entry

I trust that it wasn't your intention to:
_____
_____

I feel _____ when:
        {emotion(s)}
_____
_____
_____

When I'm _____, my body feels_____
            {emotion(s)}   {sensation(s)}

in my _____.
          {body part(s)}

I feel **emotionally unsafe** to talk with you when:
_____
_____

I'd feel **safer** to talk if:
_____
_____

Our relationship is important to me and:
_____
_____

Date: _____   Teen Entry

I trust that it wasn't your intention to:
_____
_____

I feel _____ when:
      {emotion(s)}

_____
_____
_____

When I'm _____, my body feels_____
      {emotion(s)}   {sensation(s)}

in my _____.
      {body part(s)}

I feel **emotionally unsafe** to talk with you when:
_____
_____

I'd feel **safer** to talk if:
_____
_____

Our relationship is important to me and:
_____
_____

Date: _____   Parent Entry

I trust that it wasn't your intention to:
_____
_____

I feel _____ when:
    {emotion(s)}

_____
_____
_____

When I'm _____, my body feels_____
    {emotion(s)}   {sensation(s)}

in my _____.
    {body part(s)}

I feel **emotionally unsafe** to talk with you when:
_____
_____

I'd feel **safer** to talk if:
_____
_____

Our relationship is important to me and:
_____
_____

Date: Teen Entry

I trust that it wasn't your intention to:
_____
_____

I feel _____ when:
      {emotion(s)}

_____
_____
_____

When I'm _____, my body feels_____
              {emotion(s)}   {sensation(s)}

in my _____.
        {body part(s)}

I feel **emotionally unsafe** to talk with you when:
_____
_____

I'd feel **safer** to talk if:
_____
_____

Our relationship is important to me and:
_____
_____

Date: Parent Entry

I trust that it wasn't your intention to:
_____
_____

I feel _____ when:
      {emotion(s)}
_____
_____
_____

When I'm _____, my body feels_____
      {emotion(s)}   {sensation(s)}

in my _____.
      {body part(s)}

I feel **emotionally unsafe** to talk with you when:
_____
_____

I'd feel **safer** to talk if:
_____
_____

Our relationship is important to me and:
_____
_____

Date: _____   Teen Entry

I trust that it wasn't your intention to:
_____
_____

I feel _____ when:
     {emotion(s)}

_____
_____
_____

When I'm _____, my body feels_____
          {emotion(s)}   {sensation(s)}

in my _____.
      {body part(s)}

I feel **emotionally unsafe** to talk with you when:
_____
_____

I'd feel **safer** to talk if:
_____
_____

Our relationship is important to me and:
_____
_____

Date: Parent Entry

I trust that it wasn't your intention to:

_____

_____

I feel _____ when:
      {emotion(s)}

_____

_____

_____

When I'm _____, my body feels_____
            {emotion(s)}   {sensation(s)}

in my _____.
         {body part(s)}

I feel **emotionally unsafe** to talk with you when:

_____

_____

I'd feel **safer** to talk if:

_____

_____

Our relationship is important to me and:

_____

_____

Date: Teen Entry

I trust that it wasn't your intention to:

_____

_____

I feel _____ when:
      {emotion(s)}

_____

_____

When I'm _____, my body feels _____
         {emotion(s)}   {sensation(s)}

in my _____.
        {body part(s)}

I feel **emotionally unsafe** to talk with you when:

_____

_____

I'd feel **safer** to talk if:

_____

_____

Our relationship is important to me and:

_____

_____

Date: Parent Entry

I trust that it wasn't your intention to:
_____
_____

I feel _____ when:
      {emotion(s)}

_____
_____

When I'm _____, my body feels_____
            {emotion(s)}   {sensation(s)}

in my _____.
        {body part(s)}

I feel **emotionally unsafe** to talk with you when:
_____
_____

I'd feel **safer** to talk if:
_____
_____

Our relationship is important to me and:
_____
_____

Date: Teen Entry

I trust that it wasn't your intention to:
_____
_____

I feel _____ when:
     {emotion(s)}

_____
_____
_____

When I'm _____, my body feels_____
     {emotion(s)}   {sensation(s)}

in my _____.
     {body part(s)}

I feel **emotionally unsafe** to talk with you when:
_____
_____

I'd feel **safer** to talk if:
_____
_____

Our relationship is important to me and:
_____
_____

Date: Parent Entry

I trust that it wasn't your intention to:
_____
_____

I feel _____ when:
      {emotion(s)}

_____
_____

_____

When I'm _____, my body feels_____
    {emotion(s)}   {sensation(s)}

in my _____.
      {body part(s)}

I feel **emotionally unsafe** to talk with you when:
_____
_____

I'd feel **safer** to talk if:
_____
_____

Our relationship is important to me and:
_____
_____

Date: Teen Entry

I trust that it wasn't your intention to:
_____
_____

I feel _____ when:
　　　　{emotion(s)}

_____
_____
_____

When I'm _____, my body feels_____
　　　　　　　{emotion(s)}　　　　　　　　　　　　　{sensation(s)}

in my _____.
　　　　{body part(s)}

I feel **emotionally unsafe** to talk with you when:
_____
_____

I'd feel **safer** to talk if:
_____
_____

Our relationship is important to me and:
_____
_____

Date: Parent Entry

I trust that it wasn't your intention to:
_____
_____

I feel _____ when:
      {emotion(s)}

_____
_____
_____

When I'm _____, my body feels_____
         {emotion(s)}   {sensation(s)}

in my _____.
      {body part(s)}

I feel **emotionally unsafe** to talk with you when:
_____
_____

I'd feel **safer** to talk if:
_____
_____

Our relationship is important to me and:
_____
_____

About the Author

Gina has been a Licensed Clinical Social Worker for over 2 decades and has spent the past 25 years of her career helping individuals and families learn to adapt and cope with difficult life transitions.

She is the creator of Combating Teen Anxiety, a proven 10-step method to reduce anxiety and give teens the skills to manage their emotions so they can succeed in their future goals. She created this parent and teen communication journal designed to give teens the language and tools to express themselves with their parents when conversations are difficult to discuss in person.

In addition to this journal and working with people in her private practice through online training programs, virtual coaching nationwide, and in person and online psychotherapy in California and Idaho, Gina offers corporate workshops and keynote speaking. Her expertise is in teaching teens and adults to catch their anxiety before it gets out of control, and to practice owning, speaking, and releasing their emotions in a more productive way.

As a Certified EMDR Therapist, her specialized training helps decrease client's negative beliefs that fuel their anxiety and provide them with a new perspective. Her experience as a Certified Daring Way Facilitator™ encourages clients to embrace vulnerability as a necessary step for shame resilience and connection.

Gina's clinical expertise combined with her personal journey raising three kids through their own challenges, and her son's gender transition, are what really helps her connect on a deeper level and transform the lives of her clients. When she's not helping others, Gina loves adventuring in the great outdoors with family and friends.

Learn more at **AuthenticGains.com** and **CombatingTeenAnxiety.com**.

Additional Ways To Connect With Gina

f www.facebook.com/authenticgains

▣ https://www.instagram.com/authentic_gains/

✉ gina@ginanelson.net

📞 (916) 496-7663

Let's Keep In Touch-
I'd love to hear how this journal worked for you!

Here's What People Are Saying About Gina

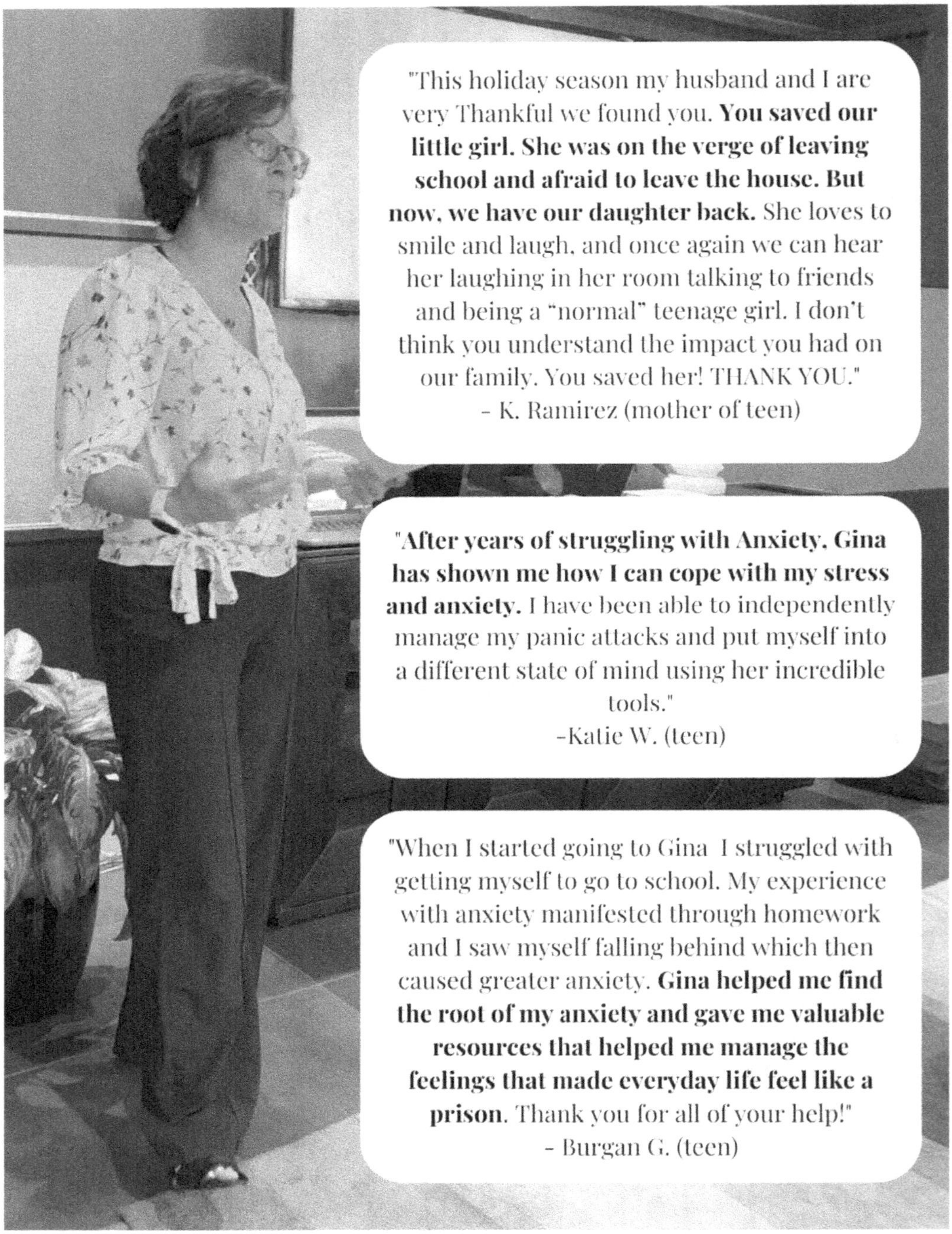

"This holiday season my husband and I are very Thankful we found you. **You saved our little girl. She was on the verge of leaving school and afraid to leave the house. But now, we have our daughter back.** She loves to smile and laugh, and once again we can hear her laughing in her room talking to friends and being a "normal" teenage girl. I don't think you understand the impact you had on our family. You saved her! THANK YOU."
- K. Ramirez (mother of teen)

"**After years of struggling with Anxiety, Gina has shown me how I can cope with my stress and anxiety.** I have been able to independently manage my panic attacks and put myself into a different state of mind using her incredible tools."
-Katie W. (teen)

"When I started going to Gina I struggled with getting myself to go to school. My experience with anxiety manifested through homework and I saw myself falling behind which then caused greater anxiety. **Gina helped me find the root of my anxiety and gave me valuable resources that helped me manage the feelings that made everyday life feel like a prison**. Thank you for all of your help!"
- Burgan G. (teen)

Additional Ways To Get Support From Gina

www.authenticgains.com

Individual Therapy and Coaching
Helping motivated individuals overcome limiting beliefs that interfere with their personal, social, occupational relationships

Daring Way™ Workshops and Retreats
Certified Daring Way Facilitator of Daring Greatly™, Rising Strong™, The Gifts of Imperfection™ curriculum in 1-Day and 3-Day retreats

Corporate Trainings and Workshops
Team Building, Effective Communication, Rising Strong™

Speaking Engagements
Anxiety, Mood Regulation, Vulnerability, Shame Resilience, Work Life Balance

Comprehensive parent and teen training/coaching
3 Day immersion group workshops, self-study course, VIP Parent-Teen Coaching

Individual EMDR Immersion Retreat
3-day Intensive to clear out negative beliefs, expedite results, and get you back to life faster

Gratitude & Acknowledgment

Thank you to my family and clients, and all of those who inspired me to create this journal to help others.

And Thank YOU! I'm here for you. Please help share these resources with others that are struggling.

www.ingramcontent.com/pod-product-compliance
Lightning Source LLC
Chambersburg PA
CBHW081749100526
44592CB00015B/2354